This workbook Belongs to :

No one is perfect that's why pencils have erasers

How to use this workbook?

There are 4 pages for each letter

1st page: is for the uppercase, trace the dotted letters by following the example of the large letter with arrows, then use the remaining space to make your own letters.

2nd page: is for the lowercase, trace the dotted letters by following the example of the large letter with arrows, then use the remaining space to make your own letters.

3rd page: is to trace letters on dotted words and sentences to learn how to join between letters to make words.

4th page: is a blank lined paper to practice what you've learned by tracing your own letters, then words and finally sentences.

bonus

The last pages of the book are dedicated to the numbers.

"Each failure brings
you one step closer
to success."

"Failure is success
if we learn from it."

"It is practice
makes perfect."

Alligator

Alli alli alli alli

Allig allig allig

Alliga alliga alliga

Alligat alligat

Alligator alligator

There are two extant

Species, American

and Chinese alligator

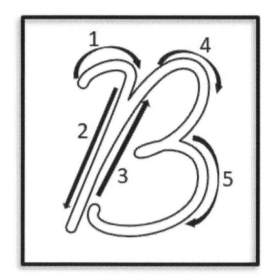

Bison

Bi bi bi bi bi bi

Bis bis bis bis bis

Biso biso biso biso

Bison bison bison

Big bison big bison

American bison can

weigh from around

400 to 1270 kgs

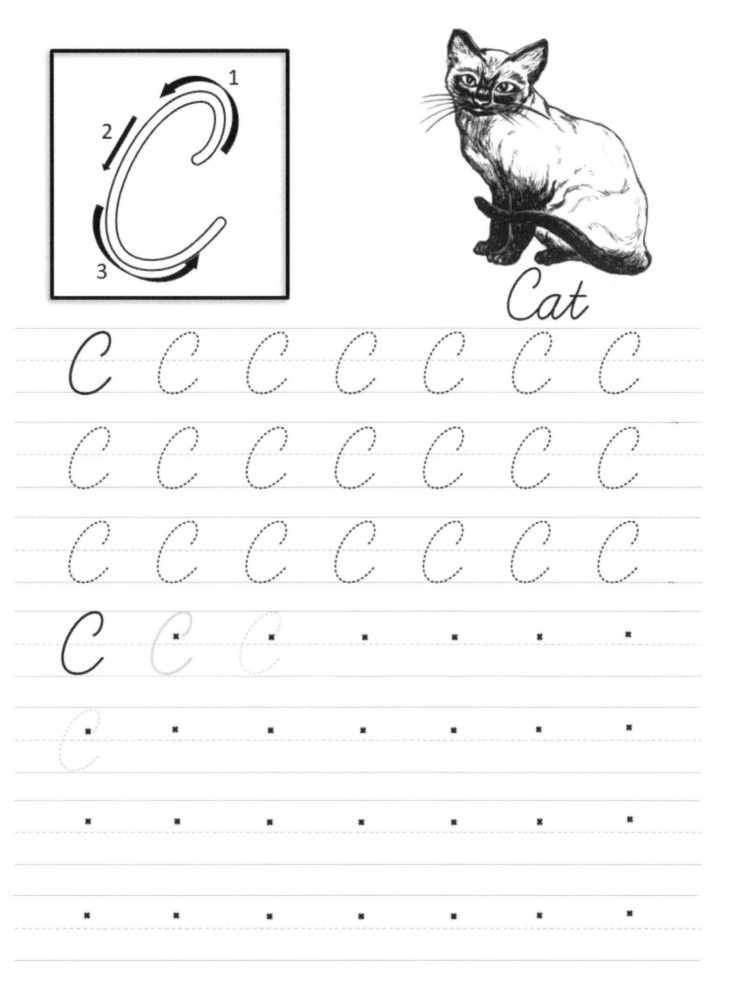

Cat

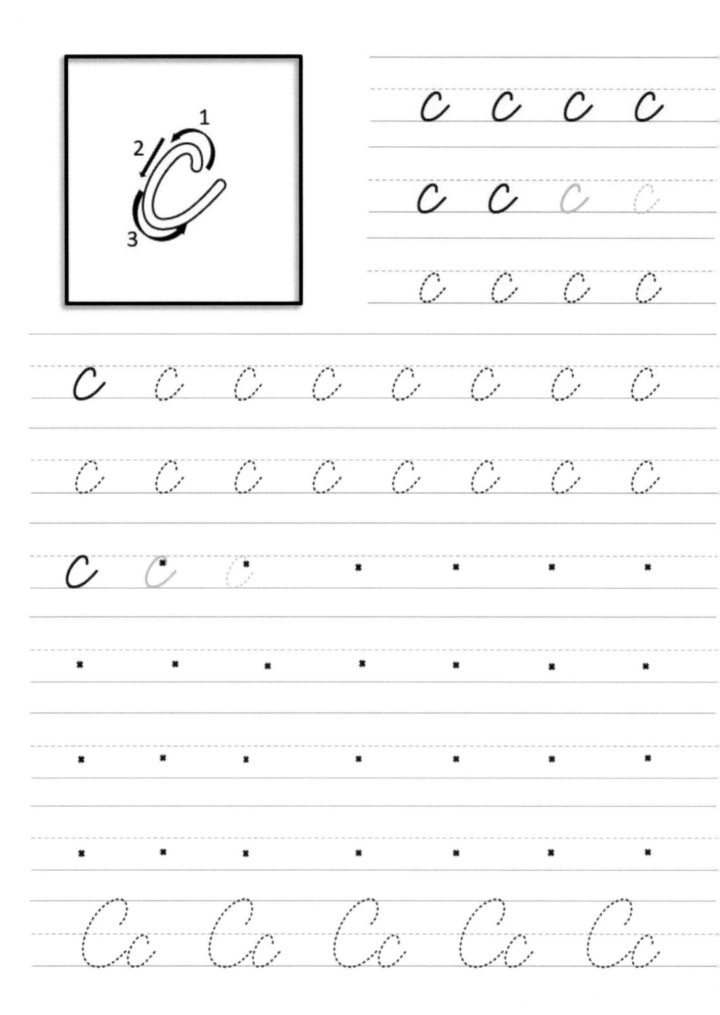

Ca ca ca ca ca ca

Cat cat cat cat cat

Cute cat cute cat

Call Cute cat

Calling Cute cat

About 60 cat breeds

are recognized by

various cat registries

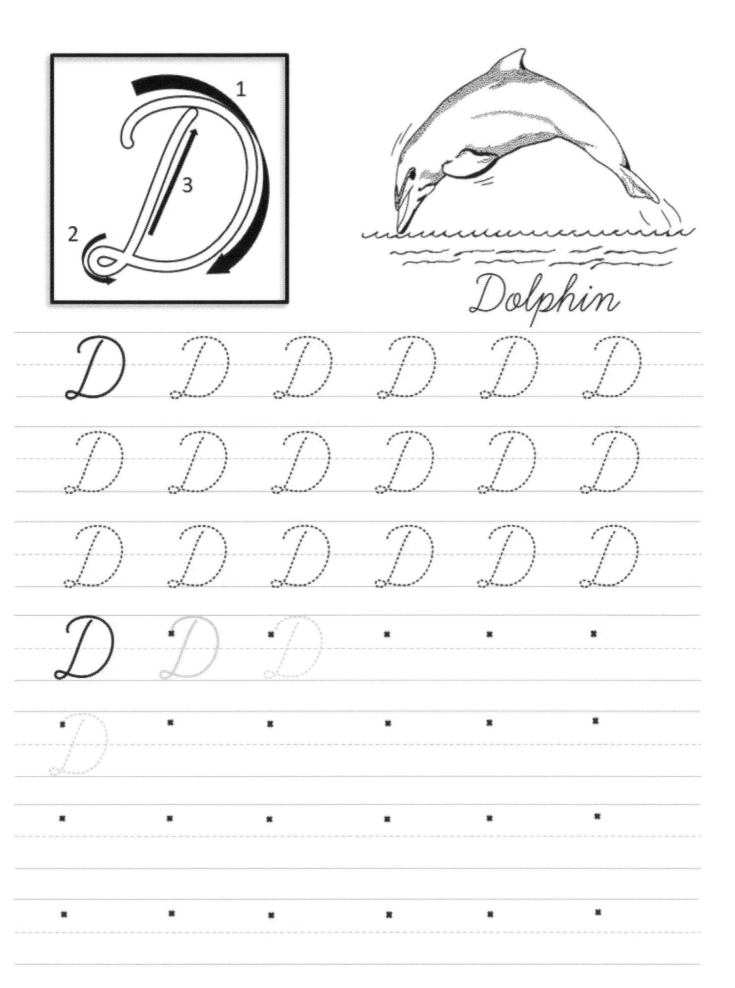

Dolphin

Do Do Do Do Do

Dol Dol Dol Dol

Dolp Dolp Dolp

Dolph Dolph Dolph

Dolphin Dolphin

There are 40 extant

species named as

dolphins

Elephant

Ele ele ele ele ele ele

Elep elep elep elep elep

Eleph eleph eleph eleph

Elepha elepha elepha elepha

Elephant elephant elephant

Listed as vulnerable species

since 2004 because of

habitat loss and ivory trade

Fish

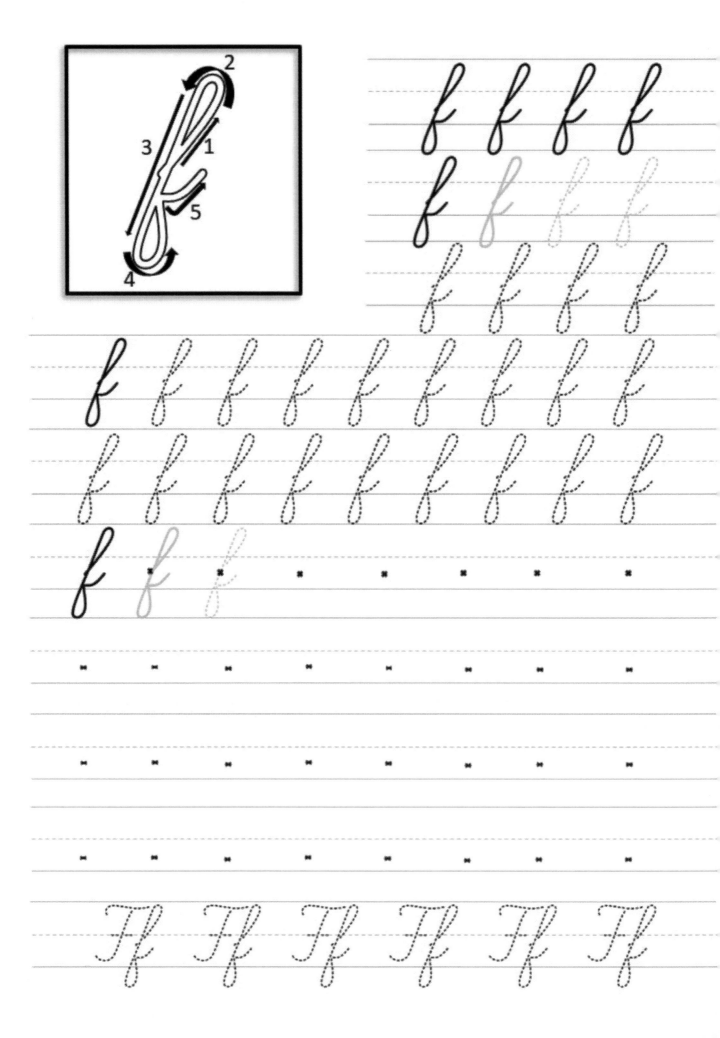

Fi fi fi fi fi fi fi

Fis fis fis fis fis fis

Fish fish fish fish

Fisher fisher fisher

Fishing fishing

About 250 new species

are still discovered

every year

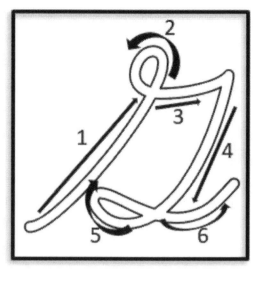

Goat

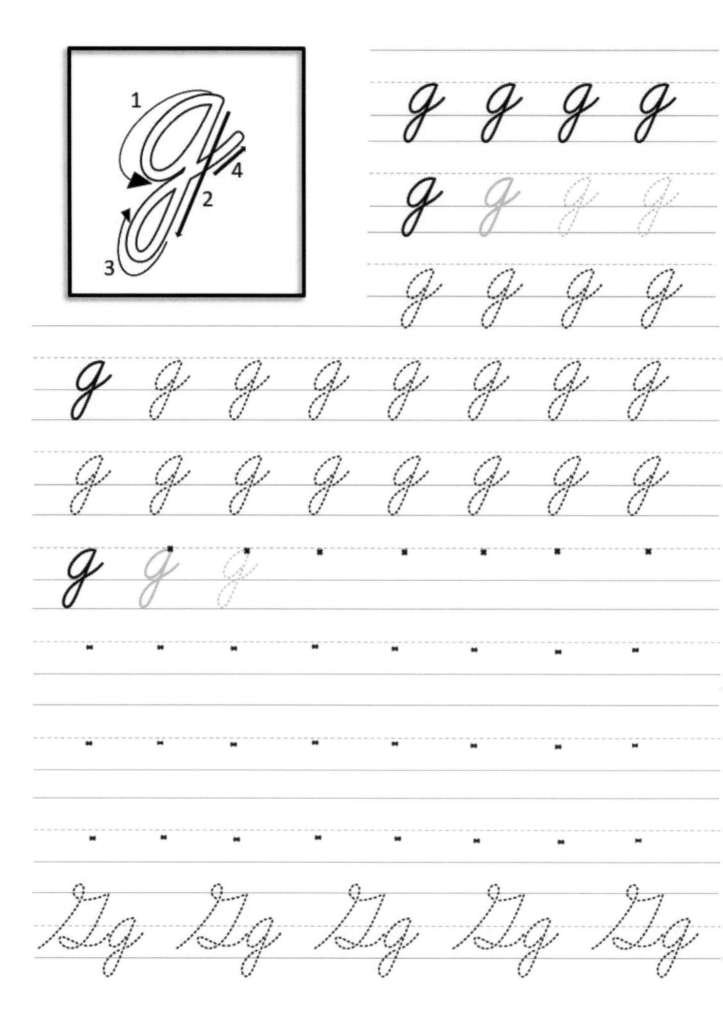

Go go go go go

Goa goa goa goa

Goat goat goat goat

Goat goat goat goat

I am gonna get a goat

There are over 300
distinct breeds of goat,
it lives 15 to 18 years

Horse

Ho ho ho ho ho ho

Hor hor hor hor

Hors hors hors hors

Horse horse horse

Horse horse horse

The horse live 25 to 30

years and can reach

88km/h in the sprint

Iguana

Ig ig ig ig ig ig ig

Igua igua igua igua igua

Iguа igua igua igua

Iguan iguan iguan

Iguana iguana iguana

Is a genus of herbivorous

lizards. The green iguana

is popular as pet

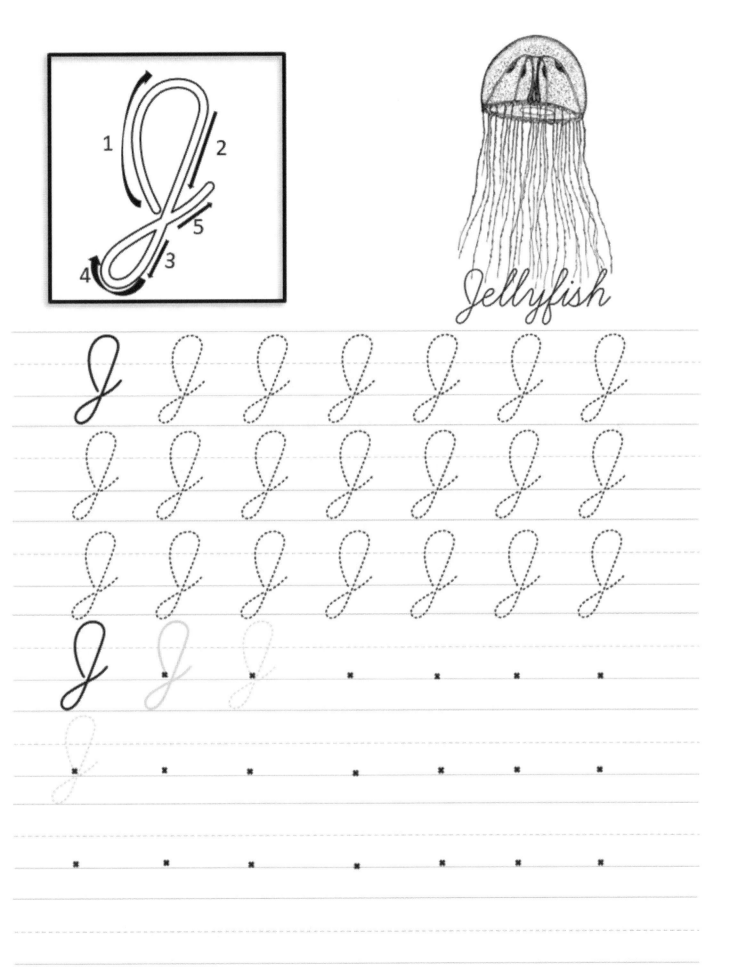

Jellyfish

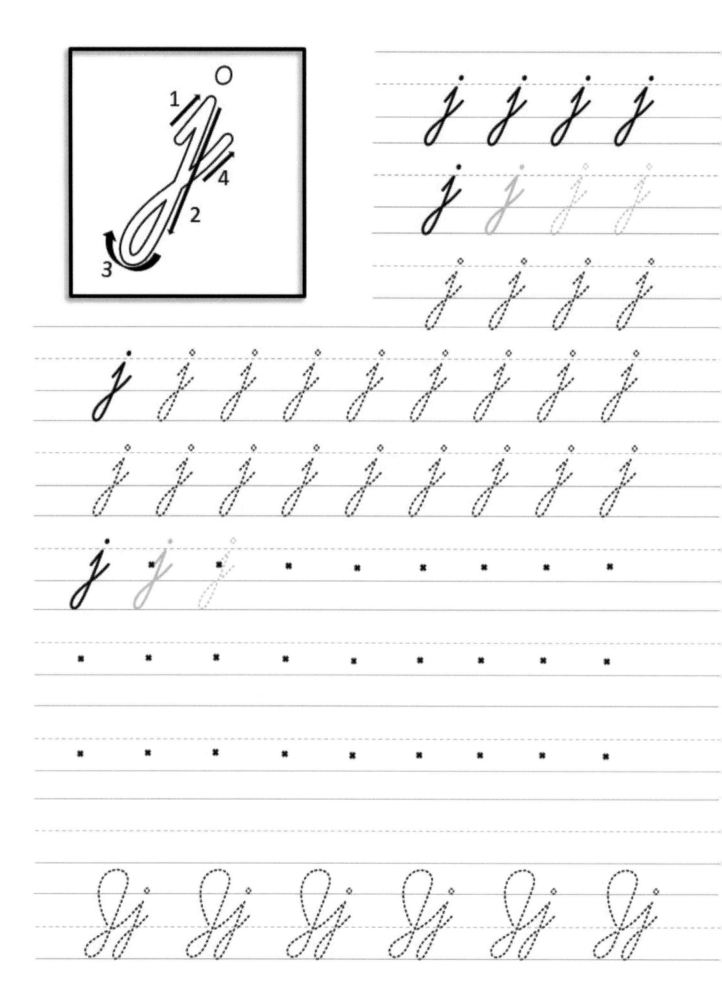

Jel jel jel jel jel

Jell jell jell jell

Jelly jelly jelly

Jellyf jellyf jellyf

Jellyfish jellyfish

Stings from few species

are very dangerous and

can be fatal to humans

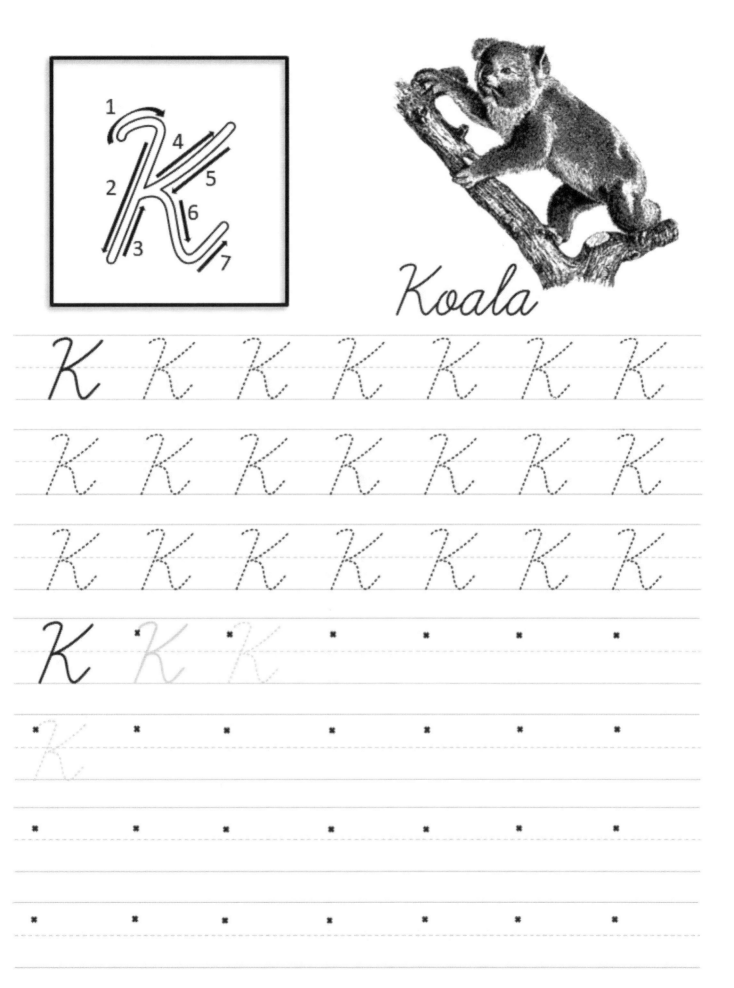

Koala

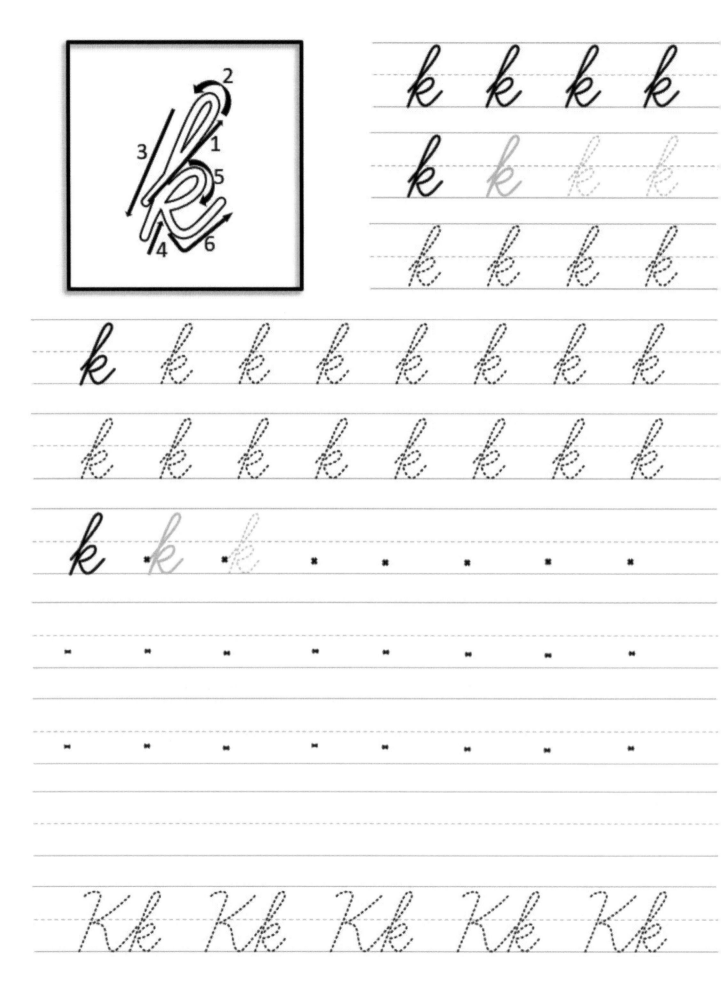

Ko ko ko ko ko

Koa koa koa

Koal koal koal

Koala koala koala

Koala likes

eucalyptus leaves

it is an arboreal

herbivorous native to

Australia

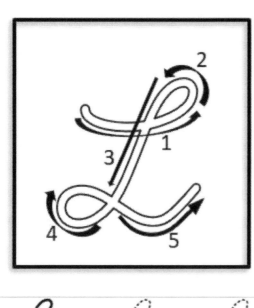

Llama

Ll Ll Ll Ll Ll

Lla Lla Lla Lla

Llam Llam Llam

Llama Llama

The llama is a south

American camelid.

Beware of the

llama's spit

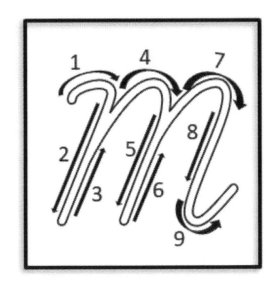

Mouse

$\mathcal{M}$ $\mathcal{M}$ $\mathcal{M}$ $\mathcal{M}$ $\mathcal{M}$ $\mathcal{M}$

$\mathcal{M}$ $\mathcal{M}$ $\mathcal{M}$ $\mathcal{M}$ $\mathcal{M}$ $\mathcal{M}$

$\mathcal{M}$ $\mathcal{M}$ $\mathcal{M}$ $\mathcal{M}$ $\mathcal{M}$ $\mathcal{M}$

$\mathcal{M}$ $\mathcal{M}$ $\mathcal{M}$ $\mathcal{M}$

$\mathcal{M}$

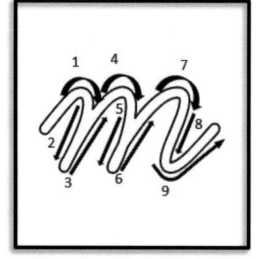

m m m

m m m

m m m

m m m m m m

m m m m m m

m m m * * *

* * * * * *

* * * * * *

Mm Mm Mm Mm

Mo mo mo mo mo

Mou mou mou mou

Mous mous mous

Mouse mouse

Mickey is the most

famous mouse ever

While the cat's away

The mice will play

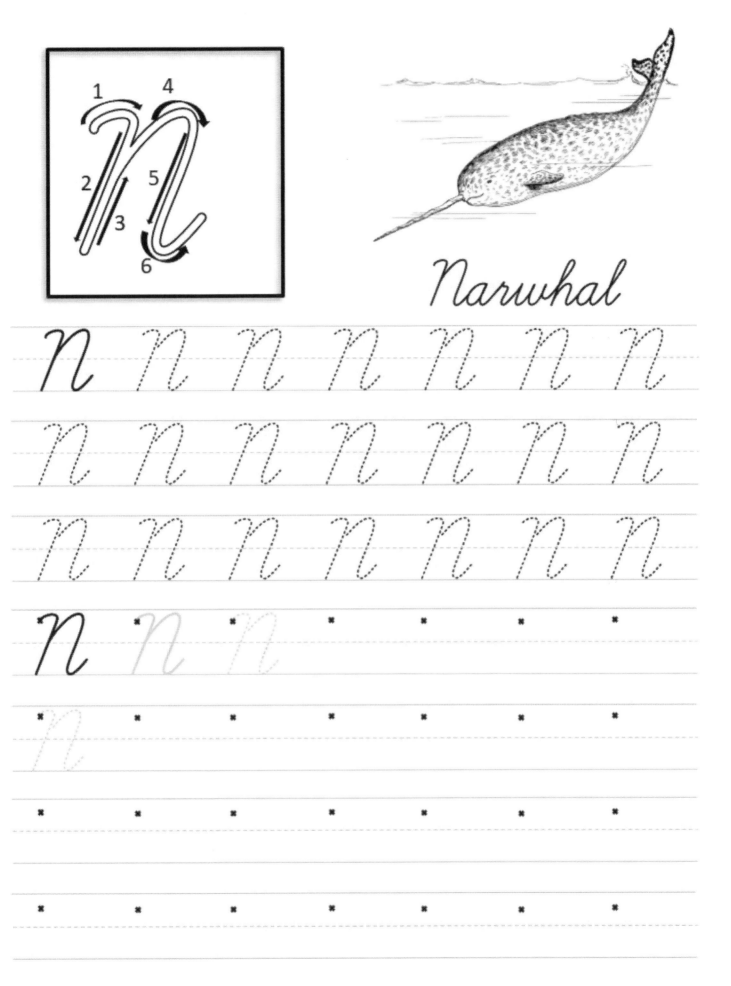

Narwhal

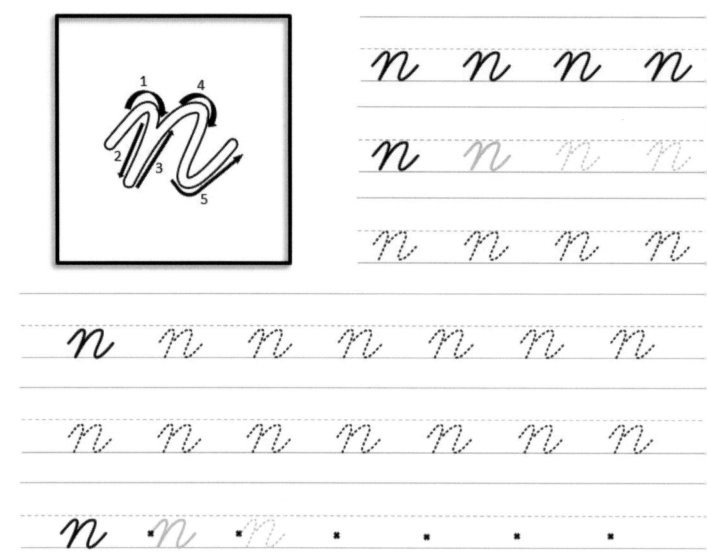

n *n* *n* *n*

n *n* *n* *n*

n *n* *n* *n*

n *n* *n* *n* *n* *n* *n*

n *n* *n* *n* *n* *n* *n*

n *n* *n* * * * *

* * * * * * *

* * * * * * *

Nn *Nn* *Nn* *Nn* *Nn*

Na na na na na

Nar nar nar nar

Narw narw narw

Narwh narwh

Narwha narwha

Narwhal narwhal

The narwhal lives
in the arctic waters

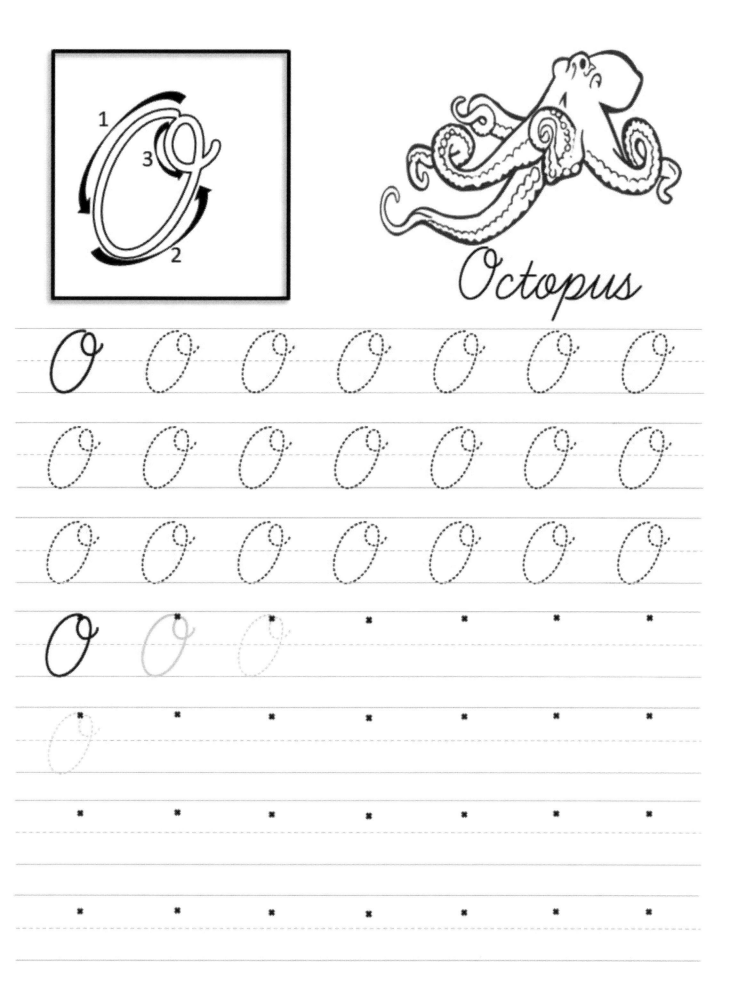

Octopus

Oc oc oc oc oc oc

Oct oct oct oct oct

Octo octo octo octo

Octop octop octop

Octopu octopu octopu

Octopus octopus

The octopus is a soft
bodied eight-limbed
mollusc

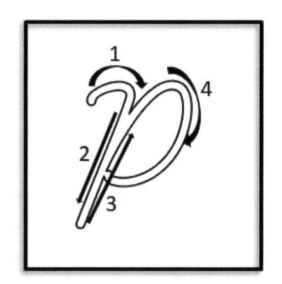

Panda

$\mathcal{P}$ $\mathcal{P}$ $\mathcal{P}$ $\mathcal{P}$ $\mathcal{P}$ $\mathcal{P}$ $\mathcal{P}$ $\mathcal{P}$

$\mathcal{P}$ $\mathcal{P}$ $\mathcal{P}$ $\mathcal{P}$ $\mathcal{P}$ $\mathcal{P}$ $\mathcal{P}$ $\mathcal{P}$

$\mathcal{P}$ $\mathcal{P}$ $\mathcal{P}$ $\mathcal{P}$ $\mathcal{P}$ $\mathcal{P}$ $\mathcal{P}$ $\mathcal{P}$

$\mathcal{P}$ $\mathcal{P}$ $\mathcal{P}$

Pa pa pa pa pa pa

Pan pan pan pan

Pand pand pand

Panda panda panda

The giant panda is

a folivore

The panda lives in a

few mountains in

Central china

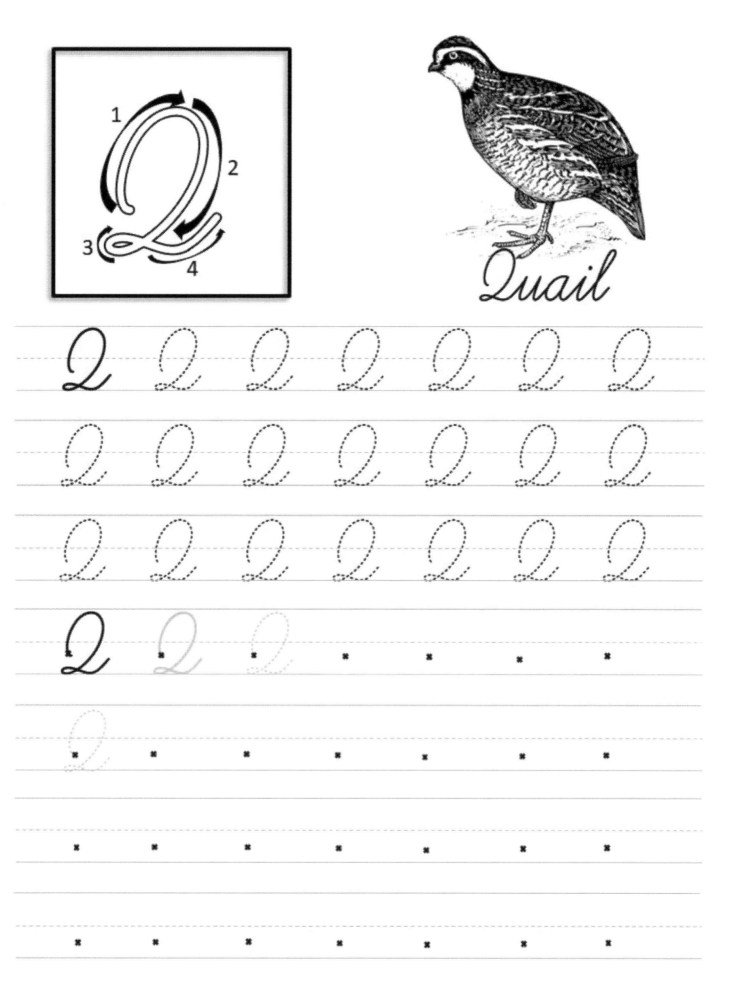

Quail

q q q q

q q q q

q q q q

q q q q q q q q q

q q q q q q q q q

q q q * * * * * * *

* * * * * * * *

* * * * * * * *

2q 2q 2q 2q 2q

Qu qu qu qu qu qu

Qua qua qua qua

Quai quai quai quai

Quail quail quail

The common quail

is a small ground-

nesting game bird in

the pheasant family

phasianidae

Reindeer

Rei rei rei rei rei

Rein rein rein rein

Reind reind reind

Reinde reinde reinde

Reindeer reindeer

Lives in the snowing

regions and also

known as the caribou

in north-America

Snail

Sn sn sn sn sn sn

Sna sna sna sna

Snai snai snai snai

Snail snail snail

This gastropod belong

to a large taxonomic

class of invertebrates

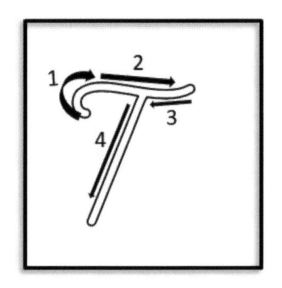

Turtle

T T T T T T T T T T

T T T T T T T T T T

T T T T T T T T T T

T T T

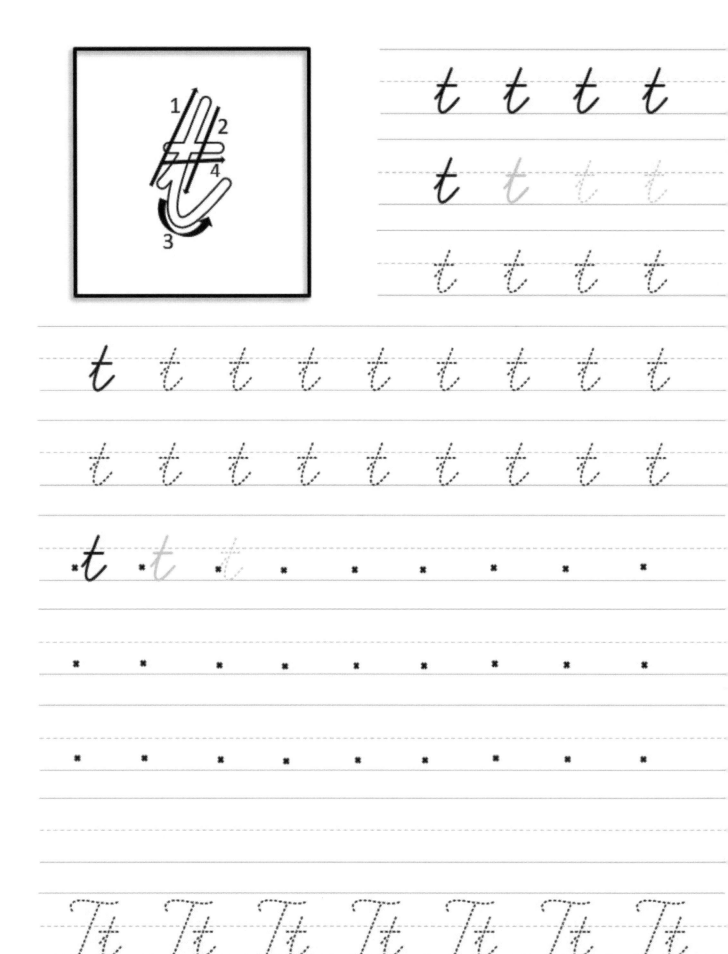

Tu tu tu tu tu tu

Tur tur tur tur tur

Turt turt turt turt

Turtl turtl turtl

Turtle turtle turtle

Turtles can live to

40 years, some species

can even reach 80

Uakari

$\mathcal{U}$ $\mathcal{U}$ $\mathcal{U}$ $\mathcal{U}$ $\mathcal{U}$ $\mathcal{U}$ $\mathcal{U}$ $\mathcal{U}$

$\mathcal{U}$ $\mathcal{U}$ $\mathcal{U}$ $\mathcal{U}$ $\mathcal{U}$ $\mathcal{U}$ $\mathcal{U}$ $\mathcal{U}$

$\mathcal{U}$ $\mathcal{U}$ $\mathcal{U}$ $\mathcal{U}$ $\mathcal{U}$ $\mathcal{U}$ $\mathcal{U}$ $\mathcal{U}$

$\mathcal{U}$ $\mathcal{U}$ $\mathcal{U}$

u *u* *u* *u*

u *u* *u* *u*

u *u* *u* *u*

u *u* *u* *u* *u* *u* *u* *u*

u *u* *u* *u* *u* *u* *u* *u*

u *u* *u* ✻ ✻ ✻ ✻ ✻

✻ ✻ ✻ ✻ ✻ ✻ ✻ ✻

✻ ✻ ✻ ✻ ✻ ✻ ✻ ✻

Uu *Uu* *Uu* *Uu* *Uu*

Ua ua ua ua ua

Uak uak uak uak

Uaka uaka uaka

Uakar uakar uakar

Uakari uakari

Their bodies are covered

with long loose hair

but their heads are bald

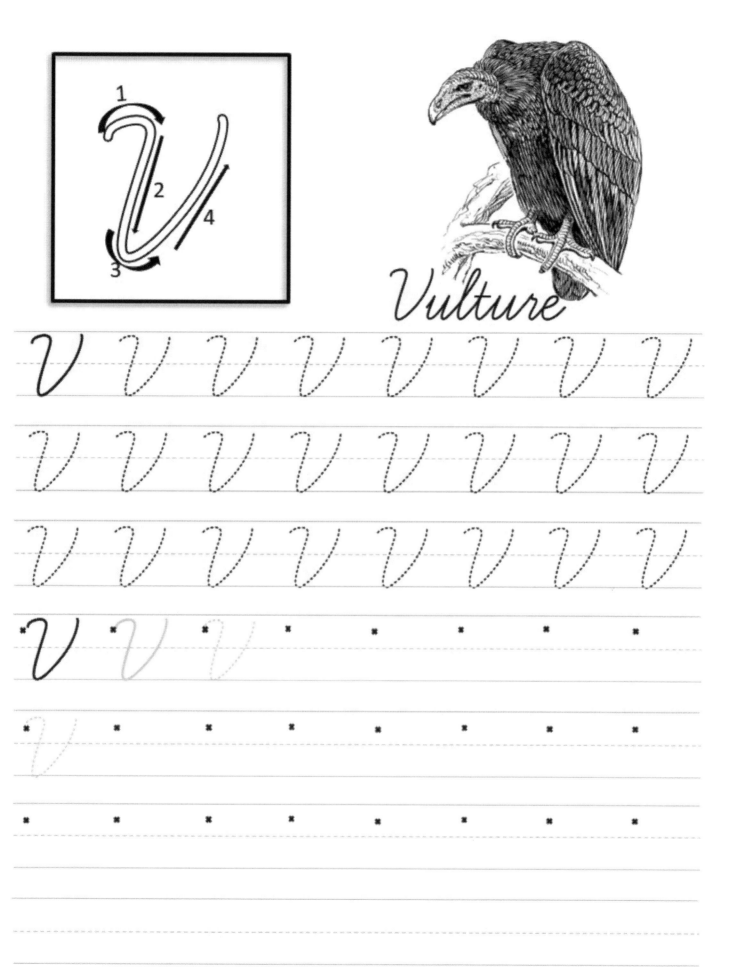

Vulture

Vu vu vu vu vu

Vul vul vul vul

Vult vult vult vult

Vultu vultu vultu

Vulture vulture

It is a scavenging

bird of prey essential

to clean the wild

Wolf

Wo wo wo wo wo

Wol wol wol wol

Wolf wolf wolf

Wolf wolf wolf

Wolf is a Canidae

Wolf exists since

almost a million

years

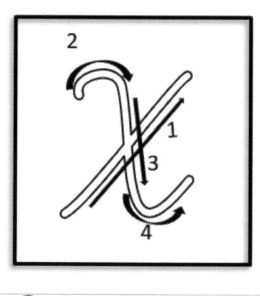

Xerus

χ χ χ χ χ χ χ χ

χ χ χ χ χ χ χ χ

χ χ χ χ χ χ χ χ

χ χ χ

Xe xe xe xe xe xe

Xer xer xer xer xer

Xerus xerus xerus

Living in burrows
there diet is roots, seeds,
fruits, pods, grains,
insects, small vertebrates
and bird eggs

Yak

Ya ya ya ya ya

Yak yak yak yak

Yak yak yak yak

Yak yak yak

Is a long haired

domesticated bovid

found throughout

the Himalayan region

Zebra

Ze ze ze ze ze ze

Zeb zeb zeb zeb

Zebr zebr zebr zebr

Zebra zebra zebra

Zebra stripes come in

different patterns

unique to each

individual

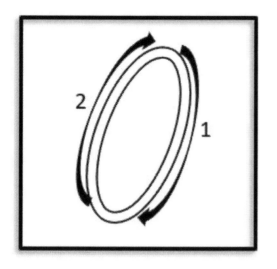

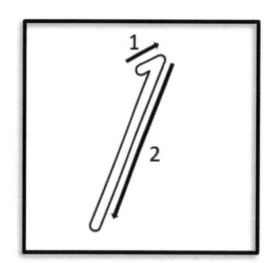

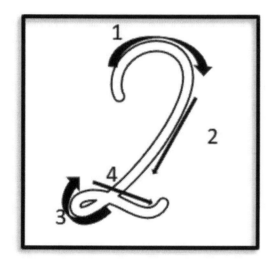

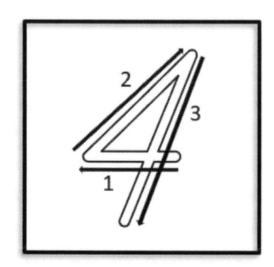

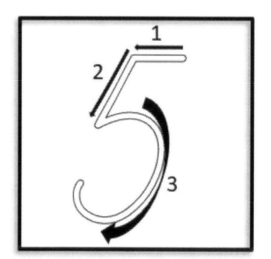

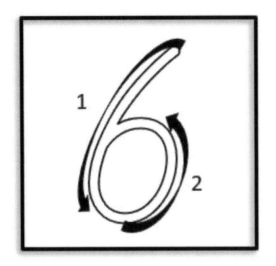
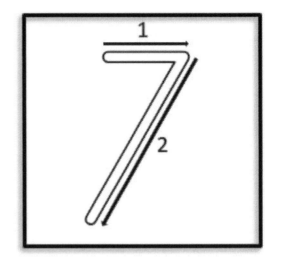
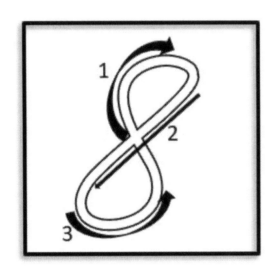

Made in United States
Orlando, FL
16 December 2024

55626498R00063